Do You Share?/ ¿Compartes?

by/por **Joanne Mattern**

Reading consultant/Consultora de lectura: Susan Nations, M.Ed., author/literacy coach/ consultant in literacy development/autora/tutora de alfabetización/ consultora de desarrollo de la lectura

WEEKLY READER®
PUBLISHING

Please visit our web site at: www.garethstevens.com
For a free color catalog describing our list of high-quality books,
call 1-800-542-2595 (USA) or 1-800-387-3178 (Canada).

Library of Congress Cataloging-in-Publication Data

Mattern, Joanne, 1963-
    [Do you share? Spanish & English]
    Do you share? = ¿Compartes? / Joanne Mattern.
      p. cm. — (Are you a good friend? = Buenos amigos)
    Includes bibliographical references and index.
    ISBN-10: 0-8368-8285-7 (lib. bdg.)
    ISBN-13: 978-0-8368-8285-8 (lib. bdg.)
    ISBN-10: 0-8368-8290-3 (softcover)
    ISBN-13: 978-0-8368-8290-2 (softcover)
    1. Sharing—Juvenile literature. 2. Friendship—Juvenile literature.
  I. Title. II. Title: Compartes?
  BJ1533.G4M37818 2008
  177'.62—dc22   2007017356

First published in 2008 by
Weekly Reader® Books
An imprint of Gareth Stevens Publishing
1 Reader's Digest Road
Pleasantville, NY 10570-7000 USA

Copyright © 2008 by Gareth Stevens, Inc.

Editor: Gini Holland
Art direction: Tammy West
Graphic designer: Dave Kowalski
Picture research: Diane Laska-Swanke
Photographer: Gregg Andersen
Production: Jessica Yanke
Spanish translation: Tatiana Acosta and Guillermo Gutiérrez

Printed in the United States of America

1 2 3 4 5 6 7 8 9 11 10 09 08 07

Note to Educators and Parents

Reading is such an exciting adventure for young children! They are beginning to integrate their oral language skills with written language. To encourage children along the path to early literacy, books must be colorful, engaging, and interesting; they should invite the young reader to explore both the print and the pictures.

The *Are You a Good Friend?* series is designed to help children learn the special social skills they need to make and keep friends in their homes, schools, and communities. The books in this series teach the social skills of listening, sharing, helping others, and taking turns, showing readers how and why these skills help establish and maintain good friendships.

Each book is specially designed to support the young reader in the reading process. The familiar topics are appealing to young children and invite them to read — and reread — again and again. The full-color photographs and enhanced text further support the student during the reading process.

In addition to serving as wonderful picture books in schools, libraries, homes, and other places where children learn to love reading, these books are specifically intended to be read within an instructional guided reading group. This small group setting allows beginning readers to work with a fluent adult model as they make meaning from the text. After children develop fluency with the text and content, the books can be read independently. Children and adults alike will find these books supportive, engaging, and fun!

— Susan Nations, M.Ed., author, literacy coach,
and consultant in literacy development

Nota para los maestros y los padres

¡Leer es una aventura tan emocionante para los niños pequeños! A esta edad están comenzando a integrar su manejo del lenguaje oral con el lenguaje escrito. Para animar a los niños en el camino de la lectura incipiente, los libros deben ser coloridos, estimulantes e interesantes; deben invitar a los jóvenes lectores a explorar la letra impresa y las ilustraciones.

Buenos amigos es una colección diseñada para ayudar a los jóvenes lectores a aprender las destrezas sociales necesarias para hacer y mantener amistades en casa, en la escuela y en la comunidad. Mediante los libros de esta colección, los lectores aprenderán por qué escuchar, compartir, turnarse con los demás y brindar ayuda son destrezas sociales necesarias para establecer y mantener buenas amistades.

Cada libro está especialmente diseñado para ayudar a los jóvenes lectores en el proceso de lectura. Los temas familiares llaman la atención de los niños y los invitan a leer una y otra vez. Las fotografías a todo color y el tamaño de la letra ayudan aún más al estudiante en el proceso de lectura.

Además de servir como maravillosos libros ilustrados en escuelas, bibliotecas, hogares y otros lugares donde los niños aprenden a amar la lectura, estos libros han sido especialmente concebidos para ser leídos en un grupo de lectura guiada. Este contexto permite que los lectores incipientes trabajen con un adulto que domina la lectura mientras van determinando el significado del texto. Una vez que los niños dominan el texto y el contenido, los libros pueden ser leídos de manera independiente. ¡Estos libros resultarán útiles, estimulantes y divertidos a niños y a adultos por igual!

— Susan Nations, M.Ed., autora/tutora de alfabetización/
consultora de desarrollo de la lectura

Are you a good friend? One way to be a good friend is to **share**. Do you know how to share?

¿Eres un buen amigo o una buena amiga? Algo que hacen los buenos amigos es **compartir**. ¿Sabes cómo compartir?

There are many ways to share. Sometimes, sharing means making sure everyone gets a **piece**.

- - - - - - - - - - - - - - - - - - - -

Hay muchas maneras de compartir. A veces, compartir significa asegurarse de que nadie se queda sin un **pedazo**.

Sometimes, sharing means doing things together. You can share toys.

A veces, compartir es hacer cosas con otros. Prestar tus juguetes es una forma de compartir.

You can share a **snack** with a friend.
Sharing can be yummy!

Puedes compartir un **refrigerio** con
un amigo. ¡Compartir puede ser rico!

11

You can share crayons. There
are plenty of colors for two.

--- --- --- --- --- --- --- --- --- --- --- --- --- ---

Puedes compartir los crayones.
Hay suficientes colores para
repartir entre dos.

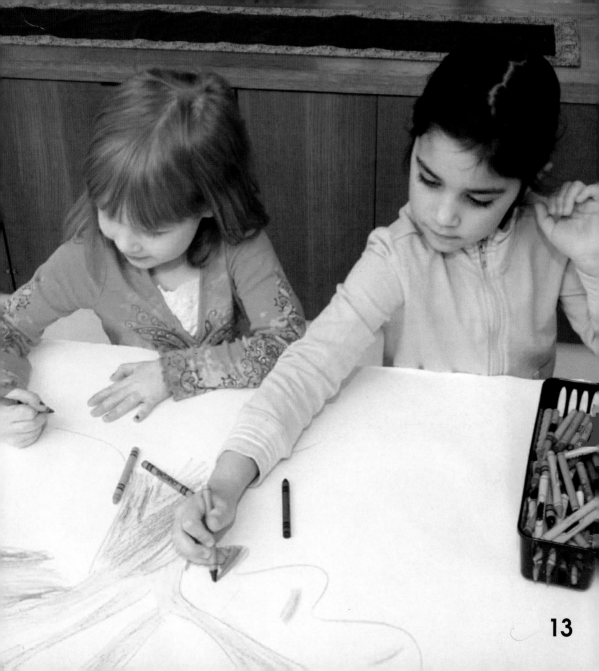

13

You can share dress-up clothes.
Playing dress-up is so much fun
when you share.

Puedes compartir tus disfraces.
Es tan divertido disfrazarse
cuando compartimos.

15

Sometimes, sharing is hard.
Sometimes, you do not feel
like sharing.

- - - - - - - - - - - - - - - - - -

A veces, compartir nos cuesta.
A veces, no tenemos ganas de
prestar las cosas.

17

You and your friend can both feel good when you find a way to share.

Cuando dos amigos encuentran la forma de compartir, ambos se sienten bien.

Sharing is one way to **solve** problems.
Sharing shows you care. Sharing is a
great way to be a good friend!

Compartir es una forma de **resolver**
problemas. Cuando compartes
demuestras afecto. ¡Compartir
es algo que los buenos amigos
siempre hacen!

Glossary

piece — part of something

share — to use something together

snack — a small meal or treat

solve — to find an answer to a problem

Glosario

compartir — repartir, usar algo al mismo tiempo

pedazo — parte de algo

refrigerio — comida ligera

resolver — encontrar la solución a un problema

For More Information/ Más información

Sometimes I Share. Carol Nicklaus (Sterling)

Why Not Share? Janine Amos
(Cherrytree Books)

Why Should I Share? Claire Llewellyn
(Barron's Educational)

Your Fair Share. You and Me (series).
Denise M. Jordan (Heinemann Library)

Index

Índice

About the Author

Joanne Mattern has written more than 150 books for children. Joanne also works in her local library. She lives in New York State with her husband, three daughters, and assorted pets. She enjoys animals, music, reading, going to baseball games, and visiting schools to talk about her books.

Información sobre la autora

Joanne Mattern ha escrito más de 150 libros para niños. Además, Joanne trabaja en la biblioteca de su comunidad. Vive en el estado de Nueva York con su esposo, sus tres hijas y varias mascotas. A Joanne le gustan los animales, la música, ir al béisbol, leer y hacer visitas a las escuelas para hablar de sus libros.